Advent: A Time for Preparation – A Time for Renewal

A Collection of Advent Sermons

The Rev'd Dr. Robert W. Seney
Professor Emeritus
Mississippi University for Women
Retired Priest of the Episcopal Church

Advent: A Time for Preparation – A Time for Renewal
ISBN: Softcover 978-1-946478-25-2
Copyright © 2017 by Robert Seney

All rights reserved. No part of this book may be reproduced or transmitted in any form or by any means, electronic or mechanical, including photocopying, recording, or by any information storage and retrieval system, without permission in writing from the publisher.

To order additional copies of this book, contact:

Parson's Porch Books
1-423-475-7308
www.parsonsporch.com

Parson's Porch Books is an imprint of **Parson's Porch & Book Publishers** in Cleveland, Tennessee, which has double focus. We focus on the needs of creative writers who need a professional publisher to get their work to market, **&** we also focus on the needs of others by sharing our profits with those who struggle in poverty to meet their basic needs of food, clothing, shelter and safety.

Advent: A Time for Preparation – A Time for Renewal

With Love, I dedicate this book to

The Mission Family of St. Paul's Episcopal Church

Mancos, Colorado

These sermons were delivered to them and it is at their encouragement that I present them in published form.

A Special Thanks

To Nashotah House, my seminary

And especially to

The Very Rev'd Dr. Steven Peay, Dean and President

Who offered me the opportunity to take part in the House's Priest-in-Residence Program, which gave me the time to complete the editing of this collection.

Table of Contents

Advent
A Time of Preparation – A Time for Renewal   9

Chapter One
Our Journey in the New World   13

Chapter Two
Listening for That Urgent Voice   20

Chapter Three
Behold There is One Among You Greater Than I!   27

Chapter Four
My Spirit Rejoices in God My Savior   33

Chapter Five
Waiting for Joy   41

Chapter Six
Watching for Joy   47

Chapter Seven
Praying for Joy   53

Chapter Eight
Celebrating the Coming of Joy   58

Chapter Nine
Anticipation 65

Chapter Ten
Waiting 74

Chapter Eleven
Preparing 79

Chapter Twelve
Hoping 86

Addendum
Advent Customs and Traditions 92

Advent
A Time of Preparation – A Time for Renewal

In this collection of Advent Sermons, you will hear echoed time and time again that *Advent* is my favorite liturgical season. For me, this season is the richest season of the Church's liturgical year. The combination of celebration, anticipation, repentance, and joyful preparation – all important themes of *Advent* – brings so many elements into our worship and into our life. I truly believe, perhaps naively, that if the world better understood and practiced *Advent*, then there would be less of a commercial bent on *Christmas*.

I have chosen to begin with the sermons first presented in 2011 to the parish family of St. Paul's Episcopal Church, Mancos, Colorado, to whom this book is dedicated. These sermons, while referencing the appointed lessons from Lectionary B of the *Revised Common Lectionary*, (RCL) are mostly based upon the poem, *A New World* by John van de Laar. I offer it here:

A New World

In the quiet moments, in the still places,
I can sometimes hear it;
An urgent voice, echoing thought the wildernesses of the world,
and of my heart,
calling me to prepare and to participate
in the new world that wants to be born.
How can I be part of something that I haven't seen?

that I struggle even to conceptualize, let alone understand?
Yet, still the voice calls, and my heart stirs.
I begin to imagine a world of joy and creativity, a world where the
poor are always cared for and the rich are always generous;
a world where justice guides,
and where mourning is always temporary;
a world where the highest values are valued most highly and where
prioritiesand agendas are set
with the greatest good in mind.
This world exists, Jesus, in the Gospel you preached,
in the stable and the cross and the empty tomb,
in Baptismal waters and Eucharistic meals,
in your constant calling, and your constant coming.
And so, we praise you for this world,
And for the dream that can learn to know it here and now
even as you do.
Amen

John van de Laar (2010) (Pages 261-262)
[Shared in *The Belltower*, the Newsletter of Christ Episcopal Church, Cañon City, Colorado] Reprinted with Permission of the Author.

This series begins with a sermon for the *First Sunday of Advent* and contains a description of *Advent* and then in the next *Three Sundays of Advent*, a portion of the poem becomes the focus of each sermon. I then added the *Advent Sermons* for Liturgical Year C (RCL), offered in 2012 and the third set for Liturgical Year A, offered in 2013. There is some duplication of content. After consideration, I deliberately decided to leave this duplication to insure continuity and transition. This repetition may prove to be a good lesson. I have attempted to reference any ideas or concepts that I have "borrowed." My apologies, if I have missed any attributions to others. I readily admit that not every thought is original. After 50 years plus in the priesthood, through a life time of reading, study, and teaching, one cannot help but be influenced by many authors and authorities in the field and the names of those influences are often lost in memory. The sermons have undergone minor editing for this publication and they stand for the most part as presented.

I humbly submit them for your enjoyment, your instruction, and the enrichment of your *Advent*.

Of course, I am totally responsible for their content and I pray I have been faithful to the Spirit of the Season of *Advent*, to Our Lord and Savior, Jesus Christ and his words, and to the Scriptures and scholars as quoted. Any errors are mine, for which I humbly ask your pardon and forgiveness. My prayer is that these sermons will enrich your life and your celebration of the special *Season of Advent*.

I would like to add a Special Note. As I began my editing, I realized that I owed my seminary, Nashotah House, Nashotah, Wisconsin more than I realized. Sermons for two of the three years are based on publications from the House. I think, then, that it is most appropriate that the final readings and editing were done while I was in residence at the House in their "Senior Priest in Residence" Program. This provided time for prayer, reflection, meditation, and time at the computer to complete this offering. Thank you to the House, Faculty, Staff, and Seminarians and especially to The Very Reverend Doctor Steven A. Peay, Dean and President of Nashotah House for providing this wonderful opportunity.

Yours in Christ,
Father Bob Seney

References

Van de Laar, John (2010). *The Hour That Changes Everything. Charleston, NC:* CreateSpace Independent Publishing Platform (September 14, 2010)

Chapter One
Our Journey in the New World

Advent 1 [B]

In the Name of the One Who Creates; the One Who Saves; and the One Who Makes Holy. Amen

The First Sunday of Advent! Last Sunday, we all indicated our surprise that *Advent* has come upon us so quickly. Where has this year gone? But here we are -- beginning a new liturgical year; beginning a new year in the journey of our faith; and beginning our preparation for the celebration of both the *First Coming of Our Lord* as the Child of Bethlehem and for his *Second Coming* as King of all Creation, which was the theme we developed last Sunday on what we call *Christ the King Sunday*.

As you are all aware, we are now using the *Revised Common Lectionary* for the lessons which we read in our services. This lectionary is used by us, by Roman Catholics, and by Lutherans, basically the so-called "liturgical" churches. In addition, many Presbyterian and Methodist Churches are using this new lectionary as well. Thus – the word *Common* in the title, *Revised **Common** Lectionary*, means that it is common or shared to and within several traditions. This gives me great pleasure to know that in many churches, in several denominations that we are all reading and hearing the same Scripture Lessons on a given Sunday.

One of the things that I have noticed in reading the lessons of *Advent* found in all three of our new Lectionary Cycles is that they are more parallel. The First Sundays are more or less pronouncements of the Second Coming. The Second Sundays focus is on the person of John the Baptizer. The Third Sundays relay the message of John the Baptizer and the Fourth Sundays relate more to the characters surrounding the *Christmass Event*, the Birth of Our Lord.

In the past, so it seems to me, the three *Prayer Book* cycles tended to develop a more specific theme which we then could relate to the *Advent Wreath*. While this is still true, somewhat, I don't think it is as obvious or as dramatic in the new *Revised Common Lectionary*.

But whatever the focus, the basic theme of *Advent* rings loud and clear. We know that *Advent* is the time that we prepare for the coming of Jesus. We prepare for the *Incarnation*, the birth of Jesus, that event in which God breaks into history at a specific time and in a specific place for the purpose of bringing salvation to all human kind. It is also the time in which we prepare for the final *Advent* of Christ in His Second Coming and the full establishment of His Kingdom.

This is my third *Advent Season* with you. So, for the third time you will hear me say -- that *Advent* is my favorite liturgical season. For me, this season is the richest season of the Church's year. The combination of celebration, anticipation, repentance, and joyful preparation – all important themes of *Advent* – brings so many elements into our worship and into our life. I truly believe that if the world better understood and practiced *Advent*, then there would be less of a commercial bent on *Christmass*.

We know that *Advent* is the first season of the Church's liturgical year. It begins on the fourth Sunday before *Christmass*, *Advent I*, and ends with the first Eucharist of *Christmass*. In addition, we recognize *Advent* as one of our two penitential seasons, the other being *Lent*. But I think that *Advent* is better thought of as a season of solemn preparation for remembering Christ's Incarnation at *Christmass* and for anticipating the fulfillment of Our Lord's promise to return in power and great glory, the *Second Coming*. Therefore, I don't think that calling *Advent* – a "little" *Lent*, which this season has sometimes been called, does it justice.

I think we should note the liturgical colors of this season. Most of us are probably more familiar with the Latin use of purple in our vestments and altar hangings, the same color as used in *Lent*, but *Advent* purple is different. *Advent* purple is a rich, red purple and not the bluer purple of *Lent*. Because of the cost of vestments, most churches use the same vestments for both seasons, which may be another part of the reason that *Advent* has been called a little *Lent*. But the color traditions don't stop there. For example, there is the old English tradition, called the *Sarum Rite* which primarily developed out of the Cathedral of York in Northeast England. Here the color used is a deep blue. The candles in our *Advent Wreath* this year reflect that tradition. In addition, last year with our new altar vestments, we combined the two traditions and we have on a background of blue a pattern in the Latin purple.

Advent is the season which is perhaps the richest in practices and symbols: the reddish purple or blue vestments, prayers that start with words like "Stir up your power;" calendars that count the days; songs and hymns and sacred songs; scriptures rife with images of John the Baptizer and his camel's hair clothing; Isaiah and his promise; Zechariah, the father of John the Baptizer and his mysterious silence; Elizabeth and her greeting to her cousin Mary; but of all these *Advent* stories, songs and symbols, there is none that is more vivid and more welcome than the *Advent Wreath*. Whether it is gracing the church's chancel, as it is here, or adorning the table at home, it is the ever-increasing light of the *Advent Wreath* – candles growing steadily shorter, light growing steadily brighter – that mirrors our growing anticipation and heralds the ever, nearer presence of Christ, our light and our salvation.

We all know and perhaps love – like I do—this symbol of *Advent*. The circular wreath reminds us that God has no beginning and no end. The greenery reminds us of God's everlasting love, and the four candles, one for each Sunday of *Advent*, clustered around the Christ Candle, reminds us that we are watching and preparing for our King. On the *Fourth Sunday of Advent*, when all four candles are burning brightly, we are reminded of the way that Jesus changed darkness into the light of joy and love and then on *Christmass Eve*, we light the Christ Candle, representing his Presence in our world. Over the years, we have added additional meanings to the *Advent Wreath* and traditionally, we have named the candles.

One of the most common tradition is to name the candles in this way: The *First Week of Advent*: The Prophecy Candle; *The Second Week of Advent*: The Bethlehem Candle; *The Third Week of Advent*: The Shepherds' Candle; and *The Fourth Week of Advent*: The Angels' Candle. For the most part, but not always, the naming of these candles parallels the appointed lessons for each Sunday in *Advent*.

Last year, we named the candles in this way: *The First Candle*: The Promise of the Second Coming; *The Second Candle*: The Candle of the Prophecy concerning John the Baptizer; *The Third Candle*: The Candle of this John, the Messenger; and

The Fourth Candle: The Birth or Bethlehem Candle. And my *Advent* sermons in the past have pretty much followed those themes which reflected our Gospel lessons.

This year, I would like to use another traditional naming and we will develop the themes of *To Listen; To Prepare; To Behold; To Rejoice!*

In addition, this year, I am going to do something that I haven't done before. Sometime this past summer, in one of the parish newsletters that I receive; there was a poem by John van de Laar, titled *A New World*. As I read and re-read it, I was struck by its obvious *Advent* theme. At the time, I thought this poem would be a good basis for a series of *Advent* sermons. That thought never left my mind, so that is what we are going to do. I will share the poem with you today and then in the next three Sundays, I will focus on the three basic thoughts that create the structure of this poem. So, this will be the focus of this *Advent* for us. Here is the poem:

A New World

In the quiet moments, in the still places,
I can sometimes hear it;
An urgent voice, echoing thought the wildernesses of the world,
    and of my heart,
        calling me to prepare and to participate
        in the new world that wants to be born.
How can I be part of something that I haven't seen?
that I struggle even to conceptualize, let alone understand?
Yet, still the voice calls, and my heart stirs.
I begin to imagine a world of joy and creativity, a world where
the poor are always cared for and the rich are always generous;
a world where justice guides,

and where mourning is always temporary;
a world where the highest values are valued most highly and where priorities
and agendas are set
with the greatest good in mind.
This world exists, Jesus, in the Gospel you preached,
in the stable and the cross and the empty tomb,
in Baptismal waters and Eucharistic meals,
in your constant calling, and your constant coming.
And so, we praise you for this world,
And for the dream that can learn to know it here and now
even as you do.
Amen

John van de Laar (2010) (Pages 261-262)

[Shared in *The Belltower*, the Newsletter of Christ Episcopal Church, Cañon City, Colorado]

I think that there is much here that can help us to truly prepare our hearts, our thoughts, and our lives in this *Season of Advent*, a season of preparation, for that is the basic meaning of this season. We need to remember that in these next four weeks before *Christmass* with its many preparations of decorations, gifts, parties, special meals, and family gatherings, we must not forget the most important preparation that this season of *Advent* demands and that is - - we must prepare our hearts to receive Our Lord as the Child born in the Bethlehem stable and to welcome Him as King of all creation.

To remind us, to guide us, and to help us in this important task, we have the many customs of *Advent* such as the *Advent Wreath*, which we just described, but the true mark of our preparations is the actions of each of our own lives. These actions will show if we are truly preparing for the *Christ*

Mass, Christmass. It is within our hearts that we must prepare through prayer, examination, and repentance to be ready to receive our Lord and Savior, the King of Creation, the Babe of Bethlehem. May God guide us and bless us in our *Advent* preparations.

Amen

The Lectionary Page: A Liturgical Calendar for Upcoming Weeks
[www.lectionarypage.net]

- *Isaiah 64:1-9*
- *1 Corinthians 1:3-9*
- *Mark 13:24-37*
- *Psalm 80:1-7, 16-18*

References

Van de Laar, John (2010). *The Hour That Changes Everything*. Charleston, NC: CreateSpace Independent Publishing Platform (September 14, 2010)

Chapter Two
Listening for That Urgent Voice

Advent 2 [B]

In the Name of the One Who Creates; the One Who Saves; and the One Who Makes Holy. Amen

Last Sunday on the *First Sunday of Advent*, I shared my thoughts with Matt as the two of us held down the fort. Of course, we had services as usual. The snow storm* did not stop us. Remember what Jesus said, "When two or three are gathered together in My Name, I will be there." So, the two of us had a great time together and of course, we prayed for all of you. Matt and I especially had a good time during coffee time as we chatted and shared for over an hour. It was a good time.

I sent my sermon to Matt and he responded that he thought it should be shared with you all, so he has forwarded it to you. I hope you have had a chance to read it. Basically, what I shared in that sermon was bit of the background and may I say "theology" of *Advent* and I commented on some of the customs that have grown up around this season. As I said then, and I will say again, *Advent* is my favorite season of the Church's year. I truly believe if the world better understood *Advent* then there would be less of a commercial build-up around *Christmass* and a more honest and genuine celebration of *Christmass*.

I also shared in last week's sermon that I would be doing something a bit different for me. I will be basing my *Advent* sermons on a poem entitled *A New World* by John van de

Laar. This past summer it was published in one of the parish newsletters that I receive. As I read and re-read it, I was struck by its obvious *Advent* theme. At the time, I thought this poem would be a good basis for a series of *Advent* sermons. I couldn't shake that thought so that is what we are doing. The poem was printed in full in the text of last week's sermon, but let me share it with you again and by the way; there are copies for you in the parish hall.

Today and for the next two Sundays, I will focus on the three basic thoughts that create the structure of this poem. So, this is our *Advent* focus this year. Here is the poem:

A New World

In the quiet moments, in the still places,
I can sometimes hear it;
An urgent voice, echoing thought the wildernesses of the world,
and of my heart,
calling me to prepare and to participate
in the new world that wants to be born.
How can I be part of something that I haven't seen,
that I struggle even to conceptualize, let alone understand?
Yet, still the voice calls, and my heart stirs.
I begin to imagine a world of joy and creativity, a world where the
poor are always cared for and the rich are always generous;
a world where justice guides,
and where mourning is always temporary;
a world where the highest values are valued most highly and where priorities
and agendas are set
with the greatest good in mind.
This world exists, Jesus, in the Gospel you preached,
in the stable and the cross and the empty tomb,

in Baptismal waters and Eucharistic meals,
in your constant calling, and your constant coming.
And so we praise you for this world,
And for the dream that can learn to know it here and now
even as you do.
Amen
John van de Laar (2010) (Pages 261-262)
[Shared in *The Belltower*, the Newsletter of Christ Episcopal Church, Cañon City, Colorado]

Today, our focus is on the first nine lines: Let me repeat those lines for you:

A New World

In the quiet moments, in the still places,
I can sometimes hear it;
An urgent voice, echoing thought the wildernesses of the world,
and of my heart,
calling me to prepare and to participate
in the new world that wants to be born.
How can I be part of something that I haven't seen,
that I struggle even to conceptualize, let alone understand?
Yet, still the voice calls, and my heart stirs.

Long ago in Galilee, there was a man; his name was John. He was preaching a new message of penitence and preparation in the wilderness of Judea. He was calling the people to make ready for one who would bring a New World. That voice was silenced by an evil king, but the message has not been and will not be silenced. Even today, we hear it. Often, in silent moments we hear in our heart of hearts, that "urgent voice" calling us to look forward to a "new world that wants to be born."

A "new world that wants to be born." Sometimes in our busy and perhaps too settled lives, I think that we forget that with the coming of Jesus that a new world was brought into being. With Our Lord's Coming, a world based on love and service to others was created. A world that is reflected in our Gospel lesson for two Sundays ago: which we summarized as *"For I was hungry and you gave me food; I was thirsty and you gave me something to drink; I was as a stranger and you welcomed me; I was naked and you gave me clothing; I was sick and you took care of me; I was in prison and you visited me."* Then the question: "When did we do this?" And Our Lord's response: *"Just as you did it to one of the least of these, who are members of my family, you did it to me."* [Matthew 25: 35-40] Our Lord created and stated an ethic of life that as Christians we are bound to live. It is our task to feed; to give to those who thirst; to welcome the stranger; to cloth those in need; to take care of the sick; and to visit those in prison in whatever form that prison may take. This is what the *New World* is all about.

But alas, we often forget that this is our task in life. But then, along comes *Advent* and we have the opportunity once more to respond to that "urgent voice, echoing thought the wildernesses of the world," and which also echoes in our hearts. *Advent* is the time in which we listen "In the quiet moments, and in the still places." This is the time in our preparations for the *Christmass Event* that we hear perhaps more clearly than ever that "urgent voice:" That urgent voice calling us to build a New World.

Last week, we named this year's *Advent Candles*, reflecting the use of the more traditional naming of the candles, as: The *First Week of Advent*: The Prophecy Candle; *The Second Week of Advent*: The Bethlehem Candle; *The Third Week of*

Advent: The Shepherds' Candle; and *The Fourth Week of Advent*: The Angels' Candle. With that naming, we can then develop the themes *Listening; Preparing; Beholding; and Rejoicing*!

So today, we are *Preparing* for a New World as we look towards Bethlehem, which shines as the city of love; the city of the birth of Our Lord; the city of the birth of Our King. Today, we listen for that "urgent voice" that comes from the wilderness: *Prepare the way of the Lord and make his paths straight.* [*Mark 1: 1-8* – Today's Gospel]

Unfortunately, this is not always easy for as our poem says:

How can I be part of something that I haven't seen, that I struggle even to conceptualize, let alone understand?

As Episcopalians, we say that we build our faith on three concepts: The Scriptures; the Apostolic Tradition; and Reason. We hold all three of these concepts in equal balance and in this way, we seek to build and to understand a faith in something which by definition can never be fully understood. God is beyond definition and beyond understanding but the paradox is that He is personally concerned and involved in each one of our lives: Even the hairs of our heads are numbered. [*Luke 12:7*]

So then, how do we "conceptualize" using the term from our poem? We don't! We take what Paul Tillich has called the "leap of faith" and on that basis, we seek to build a New World.

Today, on this *Second Sunday of Advent* as we focus on *Preparing*, we must carefully listen to the voice of John the Baptizer: *Prepare the way of the Lord.* We must carefully listen for that still "urgent voice" in our hearts. And respond by preparing our hearts, our lives, and our vocations of ministry in the New World of Jesus Christ. We know that we cannot do this unless we are guided by the Holy Spirit. So, we pray:

O Father, in this time, in this season of Advent, in which we **listen** *and* **prepare** *for both the Birth of Our Lord and for his Second Coming, we know that more than ever we must depend upon your guidance and the inspiration of the Holy Spirit. We ask that you so sensitize us that we may truly hear your "urgent voice" in our heart of hearts. And hearing your message may turn our lives to true preparation and to true ministry, in such ways that we give action to your voice to your people in your New World. For it is in the Name of the Coming Jesus, we pray.*

Amen

*Note: On Saturday night, December 3, 2011, Southwest Colorado had a major snow storm and blizzard. In places, the snow was measured by feet rather than inches. We had nearly a foot of snow in Mancos and most roads were impassable.

The Lectionary Page: A Liturgical Calendar for Upcoming Weeks
[www.lectionarypage.net]

- *Isaiah 40:1-11*
- *2 Peter 3:8-15a*
- *Mark 1:1-8*
- *Psalm 85:1-2, 8-13*

References

Van de Laar, John (2010). *The Hour That Changes Everything. Charleston, NC:* CreateSpace Independent Publishing Platform (September 14, 2010)

Chapter Three
Behold There is One Among You Greater Than I!

Advent 3 [B]

In the Name of the One Who Creates; the One Who Saves; and the One Who Makes Holy. Amen

On this *Third Sunday of Advent*, we continue our *Advent* meditations based on the poem, *The New World* by John van de Laar.

Last Sunday, as we looked at this poem for the first time, we took the first nine verses and we heard the theme of *Listening* for that "urgent voice" that calls us to the New World and then in our Gospel lesson, we heard the voice of John the Baptizer calling us to *Prepare*. Both of these themes are related to the themes of our Advent Wreath Candles, which this year we have identified as *Listening; Preparing; Beholding; and Rejoicing*!

Today, we arrive at *Beholding* and the consideration of the next nine (9) lines of our poem, *The New World*. Let me read those lines for you:

I begin to imagine a world of joy and creativity, a world where the
poor are always cared for and the rich are always generous;
a world where justice guides,
and where mourning is always temporary;
a world where the highest values are valued most highly and where priorities
and agendas are set

with the greatest good in mind.

So, with our theme for today of *Beholding*; our Gospel Lesson from the *Gospel of St. John* with the message of John the Baptizer; and our nine lines of *The New World* where do we go? Is there somehow a thread that connects these three themes together? I think so.

In our nine lines, the theme of looking for that New World, introduced last Sunday, is continued. Last Sunday, we heard about a "new world that wants to be born." In today's nine lines, we have that new world more fully described. It is a "world of joy and creativity, a world where the poor are always cared for and the rich are always generous." In this New World, justice guides. Here all actions and decisions and priorities are made based upon the highest values. This is stated in our poem as: *where the highest values are valued most highly*. I love that phrase: *where the highest values are valued most highly*. In this New World, the greatest good is the motivating factor. It is a New World of love and service. It is the new Bethlehem.

Our poet is dreaming of this New World, which he describes in the richest terms. Surely, this is the New World that we, too, wish to see and to live as a reality. Last Sunday, we acknowledged that with the coming of Jesus a new world based on love and service to others **was** created. A world based on an ethic of life described in the Gospel most simply in the terms: *"Just as you did it to one of the least of these, who are members of my family, you did it to me."* [Matthew 25:40] As we said last Sunday, this is the life that as Christians we are bound to live. It is our task to feed; to give to those who thirst; to welcome the stranger; to cloth those in need; to take care of the sick; and to visit those in prison in whatever form that prison may take. This is what the *New World* is all about.

But as we look around us, we realize that this New World is only partially realized and completed. As one of our favorite Christmas Carols says:

I heard the bells on Christmas Day
Their old familiar carols play
And mild and sweet their songs repeat
Of peace on earth, goodwill to men.

And in despair, I bowed my head
There is no peace on earth, I said
For hate is strong and mocks the song
Of peace on earth, goodwill to men.

[*I Heard the Bells on Christmas Day* is based on the 1863 poem *Christmas Bells* by Henry Wadsworth Longfellow.]

We have only to read our newspapers and to listen to the news on television and radio to know that there is no peace on earth. So, what is wrong? What is the matter? Is God ignoring us? Has He abandoned us? I don't think so. In the next verse of *Christmas Bells*, we hear:

Then rang the bells, more loud and deep
God is not dead nor doth he sleep
The wrong shall fail, the right prevail
With peace on earth, goodwill to men.

The problem lies with us – for we have not listened. We have not **beheld**, the past tense of **behold**. As John, the Baptizer says: *Behold, there is one coming after me who is greater* *than me. He is among you and you do not know him or recognize him.* [*Acts 13: 24f*]

Do you know the last verse of *Christmas Bells*? I must admit, I didn't or at any rate, I had forgotten. It reads:

Open up your heart and hear them
Peace on earth, goodwill to men
Peace on earth, peace on earth
Peace on earth, goodwill to men.

Open up your heart and hear them! I think this is just another way of saying "Behold!" John said that He was among us, but that we didn't know Him; that we didn't *behold* Him.

This is *Advent*. In this season, we must take time to find Him among us. To *behold* Him and His hand at work in the world around us. As we said last Sunday, *Advent* is the time in which we listen "In the quiet moments, and in the still places." It is the time in which we hear perhaps more clearly than ever that "urgent voice:" that urgent voice calling us to build a New World. It is the time in which we seek to truly *behold* Him already at work in building and establishing that New World.

Now is the time in which we must do more that "imagine a world of joy and creativity." *Advent* is the time in which we act in love and service to others. It is this action in our lives that informs us and allows others to know that we are truly an *Advent People*; that we are truly preparing our hearts and our lives both for his Coming as the Child of Bethlehem and as the King of Creation. This is the time in which we *behold* Him in His Glory, in His work and in His presence in our lives. Remember, it is often in the ones we least expect that we find the life and voice of Jesus. *Behold there is one among you greater than I.* [*Acts 13: 24*]

I believe this is what helps us in our *Advent Task*. Our task is to work for *a world where the highest values are valued most highly and where priorities and agendas are set with the greatest good in mind. Seeking to find the one who is among us.*

Behold, this is the New World of our Lord and Savior, Jesus Christ. It is a world "in which the greatest good" for all prompts all that we do and all that we are. May God help us to create and to establish this world and in so doing bring about a world in which *Peace on Earth and Good Will* towards all is firmly established.

Let us pray: *O Father, in this Advent Season, in which we listen and prepare for the Birth of Our Lord and for his Coming Again, we know that more than ever we must depend upon your guidance and the inspiration of the Holy Spirit. We ask that you lead us to behold His presence already among us. Help us to extend His work and His presence in all that we do in such ways that your New World is seen and known. For it is in the Name of the Coming Jesus, we pray.*

Amen

The Lectionary Page: A Liturgical Calendar for Upcoming Weeks [www.lectionarypage.net]

- *Isaiah 61:1-4, 8-11*
- *1 Thessalonians 5:16-24*
- *John 1:6-8,19-28*
- *Psalm 126*
- *or Canticle 15 (or 3)*

References

Van de Laar, John (2010). *The Hour That Changes Everything. Charleston, NC:* CreateSpace Independent Publishing Platform (September 14, 2010)

Chapter Four
My Spirit Rejoices in God My Savior

Advent 4 [B]

In the Name of the One Who Creates; the One Who Saves; and the One Who Makes Holy. Amen

It hardly seems possible that today is the *Fourth Sunday of Advent*. Next Sunday is *Christmass Day* and I think we are all looking forward to the celebration of Our Lord's Birth on *Christmass Eve*.

Next Saturday evening, we will be remembering and celebrating that on this night, the Son of God entered history. This is the One who sits at the right hand of the Father -- as our Savior and the King of Creation. He enters history not as a great king, philosopher, or sage but as an infant, completely dependent upon others. Certainly, the ways of God are strange and unexpected.

As we prepare for the *Christmass Eve* event, we look forward to fulfilling the concepts of our *Advent Wreath*: *Listening, Preparing, Beholding,* and today *Rejoicing*. As part of that preparation, we conclude our *Advent* meditations based on the poem, *The New World* by John Van de Laar. Today, we consider the last lines of his poem:

This world exists, Jesus, in the Gospel you preached,
in the stable and the cross and the empty tomb,
in Baptismal waters and Eucharistic meals,
in your constant calling, and your constant coming.

And so, we praise you for this world,
And for the dream that we can learn to know it here and now
even as you do.

Amen

This poem for me has so beautifully summarized the thrust and importance of *Advent*. It shares the *Advent* themes in a fresh and new way awakening us to the importance of this *Season of Advent* and its emphasis on preparing for the *Coming of Our Lord*, both as the Child of Bethlehem and His Second Coming as King of All Creation.

In this poem, we hear the importance of *Listening* for that "urgent voice" that calls us to the New World. A New World our poem describes as a "world of joy and creativity, a world where the poor are always cared for, and the rich are always generous." In this New World, justice guides; and all actions, decisions, and priorities are based upon the highest values and the greatest good. It is a New World of love and service. It is the new Bethlehem.

We also hear that world described as a "new world that wants to be born." In today's lines, we hear that in Jesus that world already exists. It is a New World here and it is a New World in the making. And how do we know that it exists? It exists in the teachings and words of Our Lord. It exists because of the historical events of His life: The Stable, the Cross, and the Empty Tomb. And it most decidedly exists because of our Baptisms and because of our participation in the Holy Eucharist.

This New World exists because of Jesus' presence in our world and in our lives. He continues to call us; and He makes His presence known in "the quiet moments, in the still places," in the wilderness of our hearts.

Surely, this is an occasion for *Rejoicing*, today's *Advent Wreath* theme. And where do we find an example and model of the most supreme rejoicing? We find it in our Gospel lesson for today in the example and model of the response of Our Lady, Mary of Nazareth, *Theotokos*, the Mother of Our Lord.

Today in place of the *Psalm*, we read the *Magnificat*, *The Song of Mary*. This song comes just a few verses following the verses of today's Gospel. It is a beautiful hymn of praise and thanksgiving – of *Rejoicing* – that Mary lifts to God: *My soul proclaims the greatness of the Lord; my spirit rejoices in God my Savior.* In this hymn and in our Gospel Lesson, Our Lady Mary exemplifies the total and complete response to the Will of God: *Here am I, the servant of the Lord; let it be with me according to your word.* [Luke 1:38]

This is the response that we, too, are called upon to make. This is the basis of the *Rejoicing* that must mark our lives as Christians. This is the response upon which the New World is based and brought into a new reality. This is the task of *Advent*: to remind us that in our preparation and praise: our *Rejoicing* that we come to see and know the dream of a New World even as God knows its presence and reality. As our poem ends:

And so we praise you for this world,
And for the dream that we can learn to know it here and now
even as you do.
Amen

The *Season of Advent* is so important. It is so rich in so many symbols and lessons. I also believe that this is the Season in which each of us can: better understand who we are as Christians; better understand our purpose and ministry in this life; and better understand our role in making the New World more visible. It is a world that wants to be born. It is a world brought into existence by the life and teachings of Jesus, Our Lord and Savior. It is a world that we have experienced in our Baptisms and it is a world in which we make present and celebrate each time we kneel at the altar in the Holy Eucharist and receive the Holy Presence of Our Lord's Broken and Resurrected Body.

All of this we find in *Advent*. Again, I say it: If only the world better understood and followed the precepts and teachings of *Advent* then how much richer our celebration of *Christmass* would be. How less of a commercial bent, there would be in this *Christmass* season?

So, for one last time, let us return to our poem, *The New World* by John Van de Laar:

A New World

In the quiet moments, in the still places,
I can sometimes hear it;
An urgent voice, echoing thought the wildernesses of the world,
    and of my heart,
      calling me to prepare and to participate
      in the new world that wants to be born.
How can I be part of something that I haven't seen,
that I struggle even to conceptualize, let alone understand?
Yet, still the voice calls, and my heart stirs.
I begin to imagine a world of joy and creativity, a world where the
poor are always cared for and the rich are always generous;

a world where justice guides,
and where mourning is always temporary;
a world where the highest values are valued most highly and where priorities
and agendas are set
with the greatest good in mind.
This world exists, Jesus, in the Gospel you preached,
in the stable and the cross and the empty tomb,
in Baptismal waters and Eucharistic meals,
in your constant calling, and your constant coming.
And so we praise you for this world,
And for the dream that can learn to know it here and now
even as you do.
Amen

John van de Laar (2010) (Pages 261-262)
[Shared in *The Belltower*, the Newsletter of Christ Episcopal Church, Cañon City, Colorado]

An urgent voice, echoing thought the wildernesses of the world,
and of my heart,
calling me to prepare and to participate
in the new world that wants to be born.
Calling me to prepare and to participate in the new world that wants to be born…

This is the message of *Advent*; this is the meaning of *Advent*; and this is our *Advent* life and ministry. We are not only witnesses to this New World, but we are participants. And surely this **is** the basis of our *Rejoicing*.

Let us join our voice with Mary and declare: *My soul proclaims the greatness of the Lord, my spirit* **rejoices** *in God my Savior.* [*Luke 1:46*] May God help us to follow the example of Our

Lady and to fully and completely respond to Him with our total lives:

Here we are, the servants of the Lord; let it be unto us according to your word. [Luke 1:38]

Let us pray:

O Father, in this Advent Season, we have attempted to prepare for the Birth of Our Lord and for his Coming Again by Listening, by Preparing, by Beholding and by Rejoicing. We know that more than ever we must depend upon your guidance and the inspiration of the Holy Spirit. We ask that you lead us to follow the example of your daughter, Our Lady Mary, to fully and completely bend our wills to You. May we like her, fully respond to your Will. Guide us in making your New World a more visible presence. For it is in the Name of the Coming Jesus, we pray.

Amen

The Lectionary Page: A Liturgical Calendar for Upcoming Weeks [www.lectionarypage.net]

- *2 Samuel 7:1-11, 16*
- *Romans 16:25-27*
- *Luke 1:26-38*
- *Canticle 3 or Canticle 15*
- *or Psalm 89:1-4, 19-26*

References

Van de Laar, John (2010). *The Hour That Changes Everything.* Charleston, NC: CreateSpace Independent Publishing Platform (September 14, 2010).

Part 2: Advent 2012

Lectionary C

Chapter Five
Waiting for Joy

Advent 1 [C]

In the Name of Father, Son and Holy Spirit. Amen

Today is the *First Sunday of Advent:* the beginning of a new liturgical season; the beginning of a new liturgical year; a new year in the life of the Church; and a new year for our own spiritual growth. In *Advent*, we prepare for the Coming of Jesus. We prepare for the *Incarnation*, God becoming man in the person of Jesus Christ. This is the event in which God breaks into a specific time and a specific place for the purpose of bringing salvation to all human kind. It is also a time in which we prepare for the final *Advent of Christ* in His Second Coming and the full establishment of His Kingdom.

In thinking about a possible theme for us to follow this *Advent* and to ensure that I am not simply repeating what I have shared with you in prior *Advents*, which is easy to do, I was unexpectedly given the answer. Since, I was gone for two weeks, I, of course, had my mail held at the Post Office. Upon my return, in going through a lot more mail than I had anticipated, I found a little booklet: *The Glory of the Lord Shall be Revealed: Keeping a Holy Advent with Nashotah House.*

As you know, Nashotah House is my seminary: a place very dear to my heart. I have been so heartened and pleased by recent events, leadership, and quite honestly the corrections of what many of us saw as grave errors not only in policy and practices but in theology as well. This year, Nashotah House celebrates its 170th birthday. Under what appears to be the very capable leadership of a new Dean, Bishop Edward, L. Salmon, Jr., new things are happening, such as the publication of this - the first in a series of *Advent Meditations* written by professors, seminarians, alumni, and friends of the House. I will be honest, I am fairly sure that I will be depending quite heavily on this little book for our *Advent Sermons*.

It seems almost impossible that we are once again in this special season. I'm sure you remember me saying that *Advent* is my favorite liturgical season. For me, this season is the richest season of the Church's year. The combination of celebration, anticipation, repentance, and joyful preparation – all important themes of *Advent* – brings so many elements into our worship and into our life. I say again: I truly believe that if the world better understood and practiced *Advent*, then there would be less of a commercial bent on *Christmass*.

Of all the *Advent* songs and symbols – the reddish purple or blue vestments, prayers that start with words like "Stir up your power;" calendars that count the days; songs and hymns; scripture lessons with images of John the Baptizer and his camel's hair clothing; Isaiah and his Messianic Promise; Zechariah, the father of John the Baptizer and his mysterious silence; Elizabeth and her greeting to her cousin Mary; of all the *Advent* songs and symbols, to me none is more vivid and more welcome than the *Advent Wreath*. Whether it is here in the church's chancel or on the table at home, it is the ever-increasing light of the *Advent Wreath* – candles growing steadily shorter, light growing steadily brighter – that mirrors our growing anticipation and heralds the ever, nearer presence of Christ, our light, our peace, and our salvation.

We all know and perhaps love – like I do—this symbol of *Advent*. The circular wreath reminds us that God has no beginning and no end: Alpha and Omega. The greenery reminds us of God's everlasting love, and the four candles, one for each of the *Sundays of Advent*, reminds us that we are watching and preparing for our King. On the *Fourth Sunday of Advent*, when all four candles are burning brightly, we are reminded that Jesus changed darkness into the light of joy and love. Over the years, we have added additional meanings to the Advent Wreath and traditionally, we have named the candles.

The most common tradition, perhaps, is to name the candles in this way: The *First Week of Advent*: The Prophecy Candle; *The Second Week of Advent*: The Bethlehem Candle; *The Third Week of Advent*: The Shepherds' Candle; and *The Fourth Week of Advent*: The Angels' Candle. For the most part, but not always, the naming of these candles parallels the appointed lessons for each *Sunday in Advent*.

This year in *Liturgical Year C*, in looking at our appointed lessons and discovering the theme that is developed, we could recognize and name the candles of our *Advent Wreath* in this way: The Promise Candle, The Prophecy Candle; The Candle of the Prophecy of John the Baptizer; and The Mary Candle. They remind us *to listen, to prepare, to repent, and to rejoice:* the theme of the Gospel lessons in Cycle C.

This year, I am proposing that we name our candles in a new way, which is prompted by our little book. In the *Introduction*, written by Bishop Salmon, he suggests that the real theme of *Advent* is: *"Waiting for joy."* He reminds us that C.S. Lewis, the great English lay theologian, in his autobiographical book, *Surprised by Joy*, found that he was looking for love in all the wrong places – sounds like a country song, doesn't it? Lewis was both shocked and pleased: *to learn that all of his expectations could be completely fulfilled in the person of the Incarnate Jesus Christ. Lewis learned that it is possible to "find and to be found by Him."* [Quote from Bishop Salmon's *Introduction*]

Bishop Salmon then goes on to say that *Advent* is our annual reminder that we, too, may find and be found by Him. He states: "The Incarnation is the affirmation that God has found us and is, even now making all things new."

The comments of Bishop Salmon and the meditations on this little *Advent Book* has prompt me to suggest that we name and follow the *Advent Weeks* and *Candles* in this way:

The First Sunday in Advent: Waiting for Joy

The Second Sunday in Advent: Watching for Joy

The Third Sunday in Advent: Praying for Joy

The Fourth Sunday in Advent: Celebrating the Coming of Joy

This naming not only parallels my planned *Advent Thoughts* based on *The Glory of the Lord* book but they also somewhat parallel our appointed Gospel Lessons in Liturgical Year C.

As I reviewed the appointed lessons from Cycle C, the lectionary which we began today, it was quite easy to identify the themes that are emphasized in this *Advent*. The *Collect for Advent 1* requests the speedy return of Our Lord and the Gospel Lesson responds with a reminder of the Signs of the Second Coming. *Advent 2* reminds us of the Old Testament prophesy, a call to repentance, and how John the Baptizer is the first sign of the fulfillment of the Isaiah prophecy of the Messiah. *Advent 3* again picks up the image of John the Baptizer and we are reminded of his message of preparation and repentance. Then on *Advent 4*, the Collect calls us to be prepared for His Coming. The Gospel Lesson retells the beautiful story of Mary and Elizabeth, which ends with the *Magnificat*.

So, on this *First Sunday in Advent* we are reminded that we are in a season of preparation and response. We are reminded that worldly pursuits fade and become tawdry and leave us unfulfilled. *Advent* reminds us that we must return to our original quest: a quest that is marked by a "Waiting for Joy," a quest in which we find and are found by Him, our Father and our God.

As we read our Gospel lessons, which this year seem to focus more on the *Second Coming*, and as we develop our parallel theme of *Waiting for Joy* we see that the *Advent Wreath* and its candles are a beautiful teaching tool and a wonderful reminder of the meaning and purpose of this season and the season to come, *Christmass*.

The *Advent Wreath* is there to remind us of our *Advent* tasks, but it is the actions of each of our own lives that will show if we are truly preparing for the *Christ Mass, Christmass*. It is within our hearts that we must prepare through prayer, examination, and repentance to be ready to receive our Lord and Savior, the King of Creation, the Babe of Bethlehem.

May God guide us and bless us in our *Advent* preparations as we anticipate and wait for the *Coming of Joy*.

Amen

The Lectionary Page: A Liturgical Calendar for Upcoming Weeks
[www.lectionarypage.net]

- *Jeremiah 33:14-16*
- *1 Thessalonians 3:9-13*
- *Luke 21:25-36*
- *Psalm 25:1-9*

Reference

Salmon, Jr., E. L. (2012) *The Glory of the Lord Shall be Revealed: Keeping a Holy Advent with Nashotah House*. Nashotah WS: Nashotah House. Reprinted with Permission of the Author. Used with Permission.

Chapter Six
Watching for Joy

Advent 2 [C]

In the Name of Father, Son and Holy Spirit. Amen

Have you ever noticed that about the only time we really hear the word "joy" is around *Advent* and *Christmas*? We hear it in so many forms: "*Joy to the World*, we sing." "We wish you all the Joy of this Holy Season," we greet each other. "May the Joy of this Season be yours now and all through the year," we write or find on our greeting cards. In our Gospel Lessons, we hear the Angels say: "Behold, we bring you tidings of great joy…" And even in our Collect for Today, this *Second Sunday of Advent*, we pray: "that we may greet with joy the coming of Jesus Christ our Redeemer." Truly, **joy** seems to be the most significant word for *Advent* and *Christmas*.

This year, we have chosen the theme of *Waiting for Joy* for our *Advent* thoughts and sermons. Last Sunday, we identified the *Season of Advent* as our annual reminder that we are indeed "Waiting for Joy:" *The Joy of the Coming of Our Lord as the Babe of Bethlehem and His Second Coming as King of All Creation.*

Then today as we lit our *Second Advent Candle*, we prayed that we are "Watching for Joy."

When I was teaching *Introduction to Speech* to middle school and high school students, and also in my instruction to students on writing essays and reports, I admonished and perhaps even threatened them never to use the phrase: According to *Webster's Dictionary*, blank is defined as …"

Guess what, as we look at the word and concept of joy, I'm going to do just that! So: according to *The New Oxford American Dictionary*, which I have on my Kindle, joy is defined in the noun form as "a feeling of great pleasure and happiness." Its origin is from the Middle English based on the Old French word *joie* which is based on the Latin *gaudium* from *gaudere* meaning "rejoice."

A feeling of great pleasure and happiness!

There are several sites on the internet which gives you various, actually trivia, information on the *Bible*, including how many times and the places a specific word is used. I found it interesting that at least two of the sites differed on the number of times that we can find the word "joy" in Scripture. But basically, we can easily say that it occurs 20-30 times. Mostly, and I don't find this surprising, joy is found in the *Psalms*, in which the psalmist proclaims the joy of living in and serving the Lord. Next, and I found this interesting, it is used extensively by St. Paul in his writings. Today's Epistle lesson from his *Letter to the Philippians* is one such example: *I thank my God every time I remember you, constantly praying with joy in every one of my prayers for all of you…* [*Philippians 1:3*]

Today, as we *Watch for Joy* we are reminded of John the Baptizer. Truly, he is the "watchman" of *Advent*. The *Old Testament* is not only ripe with prophecies of the Coming Messiah such as the lesser known prophecy of *Jeremiah* that we heard in last Sunday's lesson and the prophecy from *Baruch*, we heard today, but there are also prophecies of the messenger who comes before the Messiah. We heard one of these prophecies today repeated in our Gospel Lesson. This one, perhaps the major one is from the prophet Isaiah: *The voice of one crying out in the wilderness: Prepare the way of the Lord, make his paths straight. [Isaiah 40:3]* This, indeed, was the message of John. Then today, instead of a *Psalm*, we read *Canticle 16: The Song of Zechariah,* the father of John the Baptizer: *You, my child, shall be called the prophet of the Most High, for you will go before the Lord to prepare his way. [Luke 1:76]*

While we don't hear or see the word joy in this canticle, it is obviously a song of joy – it begins: *Blessed be the Lord, the God of Israel; he has come to his people and set them free.* [*Luke 1:68*]

So John, and by the way: we could easily call this Sunday: John the Baptizer Sunday, is the messenger of the impending joy – the joy for which we are waiting and watching.

So, what is this joy for which we are waiting and watching? For my special *Advent* reading, I am re-reading C. S. Lewis' book, *Surprised by Joy*. This book, one of his last writings, was written somewhat hesitantly by Lewis, since he really didn't like to be in the lime-light that much. But as he has stated, he wrote *Surprised by Joy* to respond to questions from readers and to "clear up" a few misconceptions. *Surprised by Joy* is auto-biographical and tells of the story of Lewis' journey from a childhood of being a nominal Christian - to atheism - and back to Christianity, where he became what some have termed: the most important and significant theologian of the Twenty Century. I know, that I for one, owe him much; both in my theological studies and in my personal readings and journey.

In *Surprised by Joy*, Lewis says this of joy:

> *Joy, which is here a technical term, must be sharply distinguished both from Happiness and Pleasure. Joy (in my sense) has instead one characteristic and one only, in common with them; the fact that anyone who has experienced it [joy] will want it again… I doubt whether anyone who has tasted joy would ever, if both were in his power, exchange it for all the pleasure in the world. But then Joy is never in our power but pleasure often is* (Page 18). In his book, *Letters to Malcolm*, Lewis makes the statement: *Joy is the serious business of heaven* (Page 93).

What an amazing and wonderful thought: *Joy is the serious business of heaven.* So, it is this serious business of heaven that we are all about in *Advent*. And on this Sunday, especially, we are *Watching for Joy*.

But again, as I reminded you last Sunday, that the actions of each of our own lives is what shows if we are truly preparing for the *Christ Mass, Christmass*. It is within our hearts that we must prepare through prayer, examination, and repentance to be ready to receive our Lord and Savior, the King of Creation, the Babe of Bethlehem: for this is what we are watching for as we seek joy, "the serious business of heaven."

May God guide us and bless us in our *Advent* preparations as we anticipate, "wait" and "watch" for the *Coming of Joy*.

Amen

The Lectionary Page: A Liturgical Calendar for Upcoming Weeks [www.lectionarypage.net]

- *Baruch 5:1-9*
- *or Malachi 3:1-4*
- *Philippians 1:3-11*
- *Luke 3:1-6*
- *Canticle 4 or 16*

References

Lewis, C. S. (1964) *Letters to Malcolm: Chiefly on Prayer.* San Diego: Harvest Press.

Lewis, C. S. (2002) *Surprised by Joy: The Shape of my Early Life.* New York: Barnes and Noble.

Salmon, Jr., E. L. (2012) *The Glory of the Lord Shall be Revealed: Keeping a Holy Advent with Nashotah House. Nashotah WS: Nashotah House.*

Additional Note:

Comments in this sermon are based on the comments of Bishop Salmon in *The Glory of the Lord Shall be Revealed: Keeping a Holy Advent with Nashotah House.* Used by Permission. Prompted by this book this year, we named the *Advent* Weeks and Candles in this way:

The First Sunday in Advent: Waiting for Joy

The Second Sunday in Advent: Watching for joy

The Third Sunday in Advent: Praying for joy

The Fourth Sunday in Advent: Celebrating the Coming of Joy

This naming parallels my *Advent Thoughts* based on *The Glory of the Lord Advent* booklet, but they also parallel our appointed Gospel Lessons in Liturgical Year C.

Chapter Seven
Praying for Joy

Advent 3 [C]

In the Name of the One Who Creates; the One Who Saves; and the One Who Makes Holy. Amen

Waiting for Joy!

Watching for Joy!

And now on this *Third Sunday of Advent*: we are *Praying for Joy!*

In last Sunday's Epistle lesson from St. Paul's *Letter to the Philippians* we heard: *I thank my God every time I remember you, constantly praying with joy in every one of my prayers for all of you...* [*Philippians 1:3*] Then again in today's Epistle lesson we heard: *Do not worry about anything, but in everything by prayer and supplication with thanksgiving let your request be made known to God.* [*Philippians 4: 6*]

While I do not subscribe to the idea that *Advent* is really a *Little Lent*, we must acknowledge that there is an aspect of penitence in this wonderful and rich season. In our preparation for *Christmass* and the *Second Coming*, there is a need and a necessity to do a bit of house cleaning and that requires that each of us look seriously at where we have fallen short of the will of God in our lives and then with *Joy* in penitence pray for forgiveness. We pray "with Joy" because we know that our Father is a forgiving and loving God and that forgiveness is ours if only we turn to Him in sorrow and true repentance in acknowledging our failure to live out His Will in our lives. This Joy marks our penitence in this season of *Advent* unlike our more serious contemplations and considerations of our sins during *Lent*.

I think this *Advent* approach to joyful penitence is actually emphasized on this *Third Sunday of Advent*. For if we had named our *Advent Candles*, as we did one year, the Promise Candle, the Hope Candle, the Joy Candle, and the Love Candle. Today would be the Joy Candle. Why is this so?

This *Third Sunday of Advent* is also called *Gaudete Sunday*. It gets its name from today's opening Introit to the Eucharist, which in the Latin begins *"Gaudete in Domino semper..."* Translated, it means *"Rejoice in the Lord always."* Rejoice as we know is also - joy.

This Introit quotes *Philippians 4: 4-6* which is part of today's Epistle Lesson and adds verse 1 of *Psalm 85*. Here is the full text of the *Advent 3 Introit*:

Rejoice in the Lord always. Again, I say rejoice. Let your forbearance be known to all, for the Lord is near at hand; have no anxiety about anything; but in all things by prayer and supplication, with thanksgiving, let your requests be known to God. Lord, you have blessed your land; you have turned away the captivity of Jacob. [*Introit for Advent 3*]

Now: a brief teaching moment. Sorry folks, you can take the teacher out of the classroom, but you can't take the classroom out of the teacher! Here is the question: Just what is an "introit?"

An introit is part of the entrance and beginning of the Eucharist, when it is celebrated in what we call a Solemn Celebration. A solemn celebration is when most of the service of the Holy Communion is sung and celebrated with incense and often with three vested ministers: The Celebrant, the Deacon and the Sub-Deacon.

The introit normally consists of an antiphon – which briefly states the theme of the day; then a matching verse or two from a *Psalm*; next comes *the Gloria Patri, Glory be to the Father…* and then a repeat of the antiphon. The introit is normally sung by a choir and it is followed by an entrance hymn which is sung by all.

You can see that this practice is echoed in the *Prayer Book* by the way that we usually celebrate the Holy Eucharist. However, we have an opening hymn first and then we have an Opening Sentence or Greeting: *Blessed be God, Father, Son and Holy Spirit.* Then a response by the congregation which is followed by the *Collect for Purity*: *Almighty God, to you all hearts are open*; and then a hymn of praise, which may be the festival *Glory to God in the Highest*; the *Kyrie Eleison;* or the *Trisagion*, which we are using during this *Advent* or, as we did this summer during the *Sundays of After Pentecost,* we used a canticle or some other hymn. Okay, I promise you there will *not* be a quiz later.

Now back to this T*hird Sunday of Advent, Gaudete Sunday.* If we were using the Latin Rite for our *Advent Wreath*, which we have done before, today, we would light the *pink* candle. In larger, more well-to-do parishes, you might even find rose colored vestments instead of the purple or blue vestments used throughout *Advent.* This Sunday's readings have a bit more of a joyful note than the more somber readings which we have heard so far. However, look at our Gospel lesson! It is John the Baptizer, the Messenger of the Messiah, preaching the need for repentance and ending with the prophecy of the coming of the Messiah. Overall, however, the theme of this Sunday is one of joyous anticipation of the coming of the Lord.

As *Christmass* draws near, we emphasize the joy that should be in our hearts because of what the birth of Jesus means to us. The great joy of *Christmass* is to see the day in which the Lord will come again, not just as the Babe of Bethlehem, but when in His Glory, He will lead us into His Kingdom. So, it is with Joy that we wait, watch and pray. And today, especially, we recognize that penitence is an integral part of our waiting. We wait and pray for the **Coming of Joy**.

The *Advent* concept of Coming is echoed throughout this season not only by the prophets but by the words of Scripture. At the very end of the New *Testament*, we find these words: *Come Lord Jesus*. [Revelation 22:21] This is the way St. John ends his *Revelation* and this is the way, we mark these last few days of *Advent*. *Come Lord Jesus!*

Let us pray:

O Father, we are your Advent people and we look forward to the coming celebration of the Birth of Our Lord and Savior, Jesus Christ. We pray that you will aid us and guide us as we prepare our hearts and lives to celebrate our salvation in this feast of the joy. For it is in His name that we pray.

Amen

The Lectionary Page: A Liturgical Calendar for Upcoming Weeks [www.lectionarypage.net]

- *Zephaniah 3:14-20*
- *Philippians 4:4-7*
- *Luke 3:7-18*
- *Canticle 9*

Note:

Much of this sermon is based on the comments of Bishop Salmon in *The Glory of the Lord Shall be Revealed: Keeping a Holy Advent with Nashotah House.*

References

Salmon, Jr., E. L. (2012) *The Glory of the Lord Shall be Revealed: Keeping a Holy Advent with Nashotah House.* Nashotah WS: Nashotah House.

Chapter Eight
Celebrating the Coming of Joy

Advent 4 [C]

In the Name of the One Who Creates; the One Who Saves; and the One Who Makes Holy. Amen

Our focus during these past four weeks has been to rediscover that in *Advent* we are *Waiting for Joy*. We have recalled that *Advent* is our annual reminder that in the *Incarnation*, God becoming man, we have the affirmation that God has found us and is, even now making all things new. And I quickly add that this is also our annual reminder that we, too, may find and be found by Him.

Re-finding Jesus and God has been my own personal *Advent* task this year. In this journey, in a not so unlikely place, which should not surprise us, in *Forward Day by Day*, in this past Tuesday's mediation, I found and I quote: *A flash of spiritual lightning strikes: I recognize the presence of the Holy Other. And each time God tells me: "You are not alone. You are never alone."* [Forward Day by Day: Meditation for Tuesday, December 18, 2012] Used with Permission.

"You are not alone. You are never alone." This was a significant *Advent* experience for me – another epiphany in my own personal journey, which has been the focus of my thoughts, prayers, and mediations during this *Advent*.

You will remember this year, we have been using thoughts from the little *Advent* book sent to me by my seminary as part of Nashotah House's 170th anniversary activities. The name of the book is *The Glory of the Lord Shall be Revealed: Keeping a Holy Advent with Nashotah House*. This has provided our focus for the theme of *Waiting for Joy*, and so this year, we named the candles in our *Advent Wreath* in this way:

The First Sunday in Advent: Waiting for Joy

The Second Sunday in Advent: Watching for joy

The Third Sunday in Advent: Praying for joy

The Fourth Sunday in Advent: Celebrating the Coming of Joy.

As we look at our Gospel Lesson for today, we have a hymn of joy celebrating the coming of Our Lord in Mary's wonderful hymn of praise that we call the *Magnificat*: *My soul magnifies the Lord, and my sprit rejoices in God my Savior.* This hymn is arguably among the most well-known verses of the entire *Bible*.

In our brief lesson from *St. Luke*, the stories of Elizabeth and Mary intersect. These two women take center stage and inspired by the Spirit, Elizabeth declares the fruit of Mary's womb blessed. The babe will become the Lord in a world of lords and masters. Mary then responds that she has indeed been blessed and we have her wonderful response in the *Magnificat*, which we have heard twice today in our *Liturgy of the Word*.

These words have inspired sermons, literature, music, and paintings for centuries. It is impossible to add to their beauty and to the depth of their meaning. I will not attempt to do so. But I would like to share with you portions and my sometimes adaptations of the meditation for today from our little book, *The Glory of the Lord Shall be Revealed*. And I quote as I have edited:

The most important text for *Advent* is from *Isaiah*: *Behold a virgin shall conceive and bear a son, and shall call His name Immanuel.* (Isaiah 7:14 KJV) Immanuel, as the *Gospel of St. Matthew* explains, means "God with us." How appropriate it is that the *Sunday before Christmass* is about the Blessed Virgin Mary, in whom the eternal Word of God became flesh. The Son of the living and true God was sent to save and redeem the world. Reading from the *Introit for the Sunday after Christmass Day*:

When all things were in quiet silence and night was in the midst of her swift course, thine almighty Word, O Lord leaped down from heaven out of Thy royal throne.

Mary is the place where God's transcendence [beyond us] and his immanence [within us] meet and dwell. "Behold the handmaid of the Lord. Be it done to me according to Thy word." (*Luke 1:38, DRB*) She is the tabernacle and vehicle of the Divine Incarnate. She is indeed *Theotokos*, Mother of God. It is through her faith and obedience that she surrenders herself to God's will and shares in God's saving plan to redeem humankind. Mary's blessedness consists in her cooperation with the Holy Spirit. She is prepared to bear the very Word of God, Jesus. She is the model of all Christians precisely because she is faithful and obedient and yields to the power of the Holy Spirit.

We, too, are called to faith and obedience: that by the power of the Spirit, "the dear Christ may enter in." As St. Paul teaches, we are to grow into the full stature of Christ that Christ may dwell in our hearts through faith. (*Ephesians 3: 17, NIV*) We are to become ever Christ–like, like Mary –

bearers of Christ and witnesses of God's unconditional love. Christian discipleship means bearing daily the Cross, daily increasing in the Holy Spirit, and becoming both witnesses of the Lord and vehicles of his Divine Charity. Faith and obedience follow the Way of the Cross, for that was the destiny of the Lord made flesh. There looms over the birth of the Christ Child, a dark shadow. It is the Cross, which He must endure "for us and for our salvation." He is the Man born to die. Mary's good news to us is always "Whatever He tells you, do it." As she spoke at the Wedding at Cana, and from her, we learn faith and obedience and utter surrender to God. She is our guide on this *Advent* journey and in our lives as followers of Christ.

Now in this journey, as we travel with Mary and Joseph to Bethlehem we pray:

O holy Child of Bethlehem!
    Descend to us, we pray;
Casts out our sin, and enter in,
    Be born in us today.
We hear the Christmas angels
    The great glad tidings tell;
O come to us, abide with us,
    Our Lord Emanuel!
Amen

[*O Little Town of Bethlehem*: Words by Philip Brooks; Music by Lewis Redner]

The Lectionary Page: A Liturgical Calendar for Upcoming Weeks
[www.lectionarypage.net]

- *Micah 5:2-5a*
- *Hebrews 10:5-10*

- *Luke 1:39-45, (46-55)*
- *Canticle 15 (or 3)*
- or *Psalm 80:1-7*

Note: These comments are based on and/or quoted from the

Fourth Sunday of Advent: Meditation Twenty-Two in *The Glory of the Lord Shall be Revealed: Keeping a Holy Advent with Nashotah House* by The Right Rev'd Dr. Richard C. Martin.

References

Salmon, Jr., E. L. (2012) *The Glory of the Lord Shall be Revealed: Keeping a Holy Advent with Nashotah House. Nashotah WS: Nashotah House.*

Meditation for Tuesday December 18, 2012 (2012). *Forward Day by Day.* Cincinnati, Ohio: Forward Movement. Used with Permission.

Part 3: Advent 2013

Lectionary A

Chapter Nine
Anticipation

Advent 1 [A]

[Sing *It is Well With My Soul* after the Gospel Reading]

In the Name of the Father, and the Son, and the Holy Spirit. Amen

I counted it up: This is the fifth time you have heard me say: *Advent* is my favorite season of the Church's calendar! And as I have also said before: *If the world really knew and understood the concept and purpose of Advent, then I truly believe that Christmass would be a lot less commercial than it is.* Perhaps I am naïve in this, but I truly believe it.

Five *Advents*: It is hard for me to believe that I have been with you for five years and now starting on six! It has been a wonderful experience for me and I hope for you as well. You are a blessing.

So here we are again at the beginning of another *Advent*. We have blessed our *Advent Wreath* and lighted the first candle. We have decked the altar with our *Advent* hangings of colors which reflect both the *Latin Rite* of purple and the *English Sarum Rite* of blue. And this year, we have started a new tradition with the *Chrismon Tree*. All of the symbols in gold, silver, and white that we will hang on the tree represent Christ in some way. When we finish our *Advent*, we will have a tree full of Christ symbols and then we will add color on *Christmas Eve* to represent our joyful celebration of Our Lord's Birth.

But we also know that as we prepare for *Christmass* during this *Advent Season*, we prepare not only for Our Lord's coming as the Babe of Bethlehem, but we also prepare for His Coming as King of All Creation.

In our *Liturgical Calendar, A, B, & C*, we find that in each year there is a slightly different approach for *Advent*. This year, in *Year A*, it seems that we will be looking more closely at the Coming of Christ in the *Last Advent* when He will come at the end of time, as we know it. He will come as the King, the Ruler of all Creation.

As we follow *Advent*, we find there is a richness of possible themes that we could follow, discover, and discuss. Our little rite for lighting the *Advent Candles* gives us one such set that we have used before. They are Peace, Hope, Joy and Love. We have also used the themes of: The Prophecy Candle, The John the Baptizer Candle, The Shepherds' Candle, and The Angels' Candle. This year I would like to use this set of themes for the candles: *Anticipation, Waiting, Preparing, and Hoping*. These themes were suggested to me by Bishop Daniel Martins, Bishop of Springfield, IL, who is also the Chairman of the Board of Trustees of Nashotah House, my seminary, in his letter in the *Advent Issue of the Missioner (2013)*, a publication of Nashotah House. He suggested these four themes: *Anticipation, Waiting, Preparing, and Hoping*.

As we think of *anticipation*, we find that we are remembering and even celebrating the anticipation of the fulfillment of God's purpose of redemption. We anticipate the Birth of Our Lord Jesus and His Return to reign in glory. In looking back on His Birth, our anticipation is the celebration of the world-shattering event of the *Incarnation* – God becoming man in the person of Jesus Christ. God entering human history.

I think our Gospel lesson for today, also suggests this theme of anticipation. As we wait upon, as we anticipate, the coming of the Son of Man, we do not know the hour or the day that will happen, but we are warned: *Therefore you also must be ready, for the Son of Man is coming at an unexpected hour.* [*Matthew 24: 44*]

Perhaps our greatest anticipation in *Advent* and in *Christmass* is the realization in our world and in our lives of true and lasting peace. For this is the season in which peace has been born, but then we look around us and find that the "Peace which passes all understanding" is sometimes difficult to find and see. I am reminded of the words in the wonderful Christmass hymn: *I Heard the Bells on Christmas Day* with lyrics by Henry Wadsworth Longfellow:

And in despair I bowed my head:
"There is no peace on earth," I said,
"For hate is strong and mocks the song
Of peace on earth, good will to men."

But then we sing the next verse: the verse of anticipation, if you will:

Then pealed the bells more loud and deep:
"God is not dead, nor doth he sleep;
The wrong shall fail, the right prevail,
With peace on earth, good will to men."

We have this hope – this anticipation of finding and knowing -- peace in our lives and in the world.

Recently, I have been introduced to the writings of The Rev'd Michael Mayne, just departed this life, He was the Dean of Westminster Abbey in London. Father Mayne addresses our human situation in his writings. He acknowledges the very real pain and suffering that is ever present in our world, but he encourages us to experience a life marked by joy and gratitude and to have an awareness of God's abiding presence and love. (Huffstetler, 2009)

This is the situation in our own lives – the problem with which we all deal: finding and knowing God's abiding presence and boundless love coupled with our joy and gratitude but yet finding the very real pain and suffering that a life lived in all its fullness must embrace. This is the challenge of our spiritual life. This is also, I think, part of the anticipation of *Advent*.

And now comes the reason why I wanted us to sing *It is Well With My Soul* as sort of a sermon hymn. First, it is one of my favorite hymns and I wish it were in our *Hymnal*. Next, I think it illustrates what I am going to call the *Advent Paradox*, which is articulated as: *the abiding presence of God in our World and in our experience: His boundless love coupled with our own joy and gratitude but yet finding all of this in the very real pain and suffering in our lives and in our world.*

Recently, I heard the story behind the writing of *It is Well*, which is a most poignant and powerful story of love and commitment to God.

The words to this well-known hymn were written by a Chicago lawyer by the name of Horatio G. Spafford in 1873. When Spafford wrote the heart gripping words to this hymn, he was in a very dark place in his life, but he meant these words to be a song of thanksgiving and praise to God in the midst of his deep grief and loss as a result of a series of tragedies.

In the 1860s, Horatio and his wife, Anna, lived in Chicago. The Spaffords were friends with Dwight. L. Moody, the well-known preacher and evangelist of the time. They were among Moody's strongest supporters. By 1870, with a successful career, Horatio and Anna began to suffer a series of tragedies that changed their lives forever. It began with the death of their four-year-old son, Horatio, Jr. who died of Scarlet Fever. Then about one year later, a large portion of Spafford's real estate holdings were lost as a result of the Great Chicago Fire.

In 1873, Moody was planning an evangelistic campaign in Great Britain. Horatio, Anna, and their four daughters planned to join Moody. They were eager to help and eager to get away after suffering such losses. In November of 1873, the Spaffords traveled to New York in anticipation of boarding the French ship, *Ville de Havre*. Before the family sailed, Horatio was called back to Chicago in order to attend to a last-minute business development.

Horatio did not want to spoil the trip for his family so he went back to Chicago alone and sent his wife and daughters ahead to Europe. He planned to join them later. Nine days later, Spafford's wife, Anna, sent him a telegram from Wales. The telegram read, "Saved alone."

The French ship, *Ville de Havre*, had collided with an English vessel, *The Lochearn*, on November 22, 1873. It took only 12 minutes to sink, taking 226 lives with it. Anna's last memories were of her baby daughter being ripped from her arms by the raging waters. She alone had been rescued from the debris. All four daughters died in the accident.

Horatio boarded the next ship out of New York to join Anna. During the voyage to Europe, the ship's captain called Horatio to the ship's bridge. It was there that the captain explained to him that they were passing over the spot where his daughters had perished. Horatio returned to his cabin and wrote *It Is Well With My Soul*.

[Adapted from *It is Well With My Soul: The Story Behind the Hymn* by Tina Truelove]

Horatio Spafford personifies triumph over what I earlier called the *Advent Paradox*. Let me repeat what I shared with you just a few minutes ago:

This is the situation in our own lives – the problem with which we all deal: finding and knowing God's abiding presence and boundless love coupled with our joy and gratitude but yet finding the very real pain and suffering that a life lived in all its fullness must embrace. This is the challenge of our spiritual life. This is also, I think, part of the anticipation of Advent.

When peace, like a river, attendeth my way,
When sorrows like sea billows roll;
Whatever my lot, Thou has taught me to say,
It is well, it is well, with my soul.

It is well, with my soul,

It is well, it is well, with my soul.

This *Advent*, as we meditate on *Anticipation, Waiting, Preparing, and Hoping*, it is my prayer that we will find that we too can sing with all our hearts, minds, and souls: *It is well with my soul!*

Let us pray:

O Father, as we come once again to this Season of Advent, we pray that in anticipation for the Coming of Our Lord as the Babe of Bethlehem and as the King of All Creation, that our hearts and lives may be changed and that we will truly know and live "that all is well with our souls." We know that we cannot accomplish this without your gracious help and love. Hear us, O Lord, as we pray in the name of our Lord and Savior, Jesus Christ.

Amen

The Lectionary Page: A Liturgical Calendar for Upcoming Weeks [www.lectionarypage.net]

- *Isaiah 2:1-5*
- *Romans 13:11-14*
- *Matthew 24:36-44*
- *Psalm 122*

References

Huffstetler, Joel W. (2009) *Gratitude and Grace: The Writings of Michael Mayne*. Lanham, Maryland: University Press of America.

Truelove, Tina (2015). *It is Well With My Soul: The Story Behind the Hymn.*
[http://www.tinatruelove.com/2015/11/horatio-spafford.html]

It is Well With My Soul
By Horatio G. Spafford, 1873

1. When peace, like a river, attendeth my way,
When sorrows like sea billows roll;
Whatever my lot, Thou has taught me to say,
It is well, it is well, with my soul.

Refrain:
It is well, with my soul,
It is well, it is well, with my soul.

2. Though Satan should buffet, though trials should come,
Let this blest assurance control,
That Christ has regarded my helpless estate,
And hath shed His own blood for my soul.

3. My sin, oh, the bliss of this glorious thought!
My sin, not in part but the whole,
Is nailed to the cross, and I bear it no more,
Praise the Lord, praise the Lord, O my soul!

4. For me, be it Christ, be it Christ hence to live:
If Jordan above me shall roll,
No pang shall be mine, for in death as in life
Thou wilt whisper Thy peace to my soul.

5. But, Lord, 'tis for Thee, for Thy coming we wait,
The sky, not the grave, is our goal;
Oh, trump of the angel! Oh, voice of the Lord!
Blessed hope, blessed rest of my soul!

6. And Lord, haste the day when my faith shall be sight,
The clouds be rolled back as a scroll;
The trump shall resound, and the Lord shall descend,
Even so, it is well with my soul.

I Heard the Bells on Christmas Day
By Henry Wadsworth Longfellow

I Heard the Bells on Christmas Day
Their old familiar carols play,
And wild and sweet the words repeat
Of peace on earth, good will to men.

I thought how, as the day had come,
The belfries of all Christendom
Had rolled along the unbroken song
Of peace on earth, good will to men.

And in despair I bowed my head:
"There is no peace on earth," I said,
"For hate is strong and mocks the song
Of peace on earth, good will to men."

Then pealed the bells more loud and deep:
"God is not dead, nor doth he sleep;
The wrong shall fail, the right prevail,
With peace on earth, good will to men."

Till, ringing singing, on its way,
The world revolved from night to day,
A voice, a chime, a chant sublime,
Of peace on earth, good will to men!

Chapter Ten
Waiting

Advent 2 [A]

In the Name of the Father, and the Son, and the Holy Spirit. Amen

We have noted in our celebration of *Advent* the richness of many possible themes that we could follow, discover, and discuss. The best example is right here in our *Advent Wreath*. Over the past five *Advents* that I have been with you, I have selected different themes for each of the candles: some from tradition and some from my current reading or some other inspiration, such as the poem: *A New World* by Jon van da Laar that we used two years ago. Last Sunday, we identified this set of themes for the candles: *Anticipation, Waiting, Preparing, and Hoping*. These themes were suggested by Bishop Daniel Martins, Bishop of Springfield, IL, who is also the Chairman of the Board of Trustees of Nashotah House, my seminary. In his letter in the *Advent Issue of the Missioner* (2013), a seasonal publication from Nashotah House, he set forth these themes and I readily admit that some of my comments come from his letter.

Last week, we dealt with the theme of *Anticipation*. We found that as we think of *anticipation*, we remember and celebrate the anticipation of the fulfillment of God's purpose of redemption. We anticipate the birth of Our Lord Jesus and His return to reign in glory. In looking back on His Birth, the *Christmass Event*, our anticipation is the celebration of the world-shattering event of the *Incarnation* – God becoming man in the person of Jesus Christ. God entering human history.

This week our theme is *Waiting*. I think this is the hardest of all of these four themes to follow and to do. Waiting is always a challenge and for some of us it actually may be our undoing! I'm sure we all remember as a child how hard it was to wait until *Christmass Morning* to find out what our special gift under the tree was. So secretly, we probed, prodded and shook and more often than not, we could guess what the gift was and thus we robbed ourselves of the delight of discovery on *Christmass Morning* when we finally were able to unwrap the gift. We stole from ourselves the gift of surprise.

As adults, we do the same sort of thing, but only in different ways. For example: today, we are conditioned by technology, TV, and the world to expect instant gratification. We want it and we want it now! Technology advances, such as our every growing smarter cell phones, have dramatically reduced the number of occasions that require us to wait. When an event occurs across the world from us, we often become eye witness to whatever is happening through television and instant communication. Today, most parents know the gender of their unborn child before he or she is born! We have become accustomed to getting and to wanting it now.

So, when we find ourselves in a situation where there is nothing to do but wait, it can be frustrating. However, *Advent* can teach us a very important lesson. This waiting can become an opportunity to cultivate the virtue of patience and patience in turn contributes to our growth in holiness. [The three previous paragraphs are a rephrasing of Martins' Letter (2013)]

Then along comes our Gospel Lesson about John the Baptizer. Among other things, his message was a message of waiting. The people of Israel had been looking for – waiting if you will – the Messiah. Especially in these times of the harsh Roman rule.

Then: *In those days, John the Baptist appeared in the wilderness of Judea, proclaiming, "Repent for the kingdom of heaven has come near."* [*Matthew 1:3*] Perhaps, the time of waiting was finally over! Perhaps, the prophecies found in Scriptures were to be fulfilled! Certainly, one of the prophecies as proclaimed by St. Matthew is fulfilled in that the messenger who was to be: *The voice of one crying out in the wilderness: Prepare the way of the Lord, make his paths straight* [*Matthew 3:3*] has been realized in the person of John the Baptizer. But even John tells the people that they must wait a bit longer: *...but one who is more powerful than I is coming after me.* [*Matthew 3:11*]

Waiting is hard and then there is the question that we all ask: But what do we do as we wait? The *Advent* lesson is that we don't do anything at all! That is the point!

We all know there are several kinds of prayer. There are prayers of actions. There are prayers of words. There are meditative prayers, and then -- there are the hardest prayers of all: prayers in which we simply sit and listen, in which we listen for the voice or will of God. In this kind of prayer, we must quiet the cacophony of our busy lives and busy minds. We must clear all that away and open ourselves to listening and this takes -- waiting. Sometimes waiting for a long time, but then, this is what I think *Advent* is all about.

Among other things, *Advent* is reminding us to not get so busy with stuff – the busy stuff of our lives or perhaps – our *Christmass* preparation. It is time for us to admit – that we don't listen for the peace of this season; for the real meaning of this season; for the voice and will of God in our lives.

Waiting is hard, but it is one of the things that we must do as we truly prepare for *Christmass* both in the Birth of Our Lord and Savior Jesus Christ and in His coming again at the last times.

I challenge you to find the time, especially during this *Second Week of Advent,* to sit somewhere quietly and wait – clear your hearts and your minds; forget about the busy stuff of your life; and the noise of our World and wait to hear the voice of God coming through. It is there, but too often we "don't have ears to hear."

Let us pray:

O Father, as we come once again to this Season of Advent, we pray that in anticipation for the Coming of Our Lord as the Babe of Bethlehem and as the King of All Creation, that our hearts and lives may be changed and that we will learn to truly wait for your voice, your will and your peace. Guide us in this most difficult of tasks – waiting. We know that we cannot accomplish this without your gracious help and love. Hear us, O Lord, as we pray in the name of our Lord and Savior, Jesus Christ.

Amen

The Lectionary Page: A Liturgical Calendar for Upcoming Weeks [www.lectionarypage.net]

- *Isaiah 11:1-10*
- *Romans 15:4-13*
- *Matthew 3:1-12*
- *Psalm 72:1-7, 18-19*

References

Martins, Daniel (2013). Letter from the Chair of the Board of Trustees in the *Advent Issue of the Missioner (Vol 30:2). Nashotah, Wisconsin: Nashotah House.* Used by permission.

Chapter Eleven
Preparing

Advent 3 [A]

In the Name of the Father, and the Son, and the Holy Spirit. Amen

As we celebrate and follow *Advent*, I have suggested many times that there is a richness of possible themes that we could follow, discover, and discuss. We have noted that perhaps the best example of these rich resources is here in our *Advent Wreath*. We continue today to build our thoughts around the themes that we have chosen for each candle this year: *Anticipation, Waiting, Preparing, and Hoping*.

On the *First Sunday of Advent* our theme was *Anticipation*. In the *Anticipation* theme, we found that we both remember and celebrate the fulfillment of God's purpose of redemption. We anticipate the birth of Our Lord Jesus and His return to reign in glory. In looking back on His Birth, the *Christmass Event*, our anticipation is the celebration of the world-shattering event of the *Incarnation* – God becoming man in the person of Jesus Christ. God entering human history.

Then last week our theme was *Waiting*, and we pretty much agreed that this is probably the hardest of all of our four themes to follow and to do. When we find ourselves in a situation where there is nothing to do but wait, it is usually frustrating. However, *Advent* teaches us a lesson that this waiting can become an opportunity to cultivate the virtue of patience and patience in turn contributes to our growth in holiness. Then in our after-the-sermon discussion, we realized that we might first need to work on the basics of trust and belief in order to be able to wait in the richest possible way.

Today, we lit the third candle, and as we can see the wreath is becoming brighter and brighter as we approach the Birth of Light, Jesus, Our Lord, our theme is *Preparing*. We know that *Advent* itself is the season of preparation, so what is the special focus or lesson that we should learn as we look into the flame of this third candle?

As waiting may be the hardest thing for us to do, preparing is the theme that requires the most effort: both physically and spiritually.

Most of us at one time or the other has painted a house, done a major renovation or perhaps refinished a cherished piece of furniture. I think Jennylynn and Jay could teach us some lessons here. I think we can all agree that the most difficult, the most time consuming, the hardest part of the project is the preparation. This may take days, and if you work at my work rate, even weeks to do. Let's take an example: if you have ever painted a house, you probably followed this sequence of events:

- First, you might have power sprayed the house;

- Then as you waited for the house to dry, usually pretty quickly, you gathered your tools.

- Then you began that long, tedious, hard, boring, difficult job of scraping and sanding off the old paint, especially where it is pealing. Koko can teach us some lessons here.

- Then perhaps, a second power spraying to remove the dust, paint flakes, etc.

- While the house is drying, this time as you wait - you begin to tape the windows, any special features or decorations, and whatever else your house may require. A time-consuming task, but it is important and it often time saving in the long-run.

- Then finally, you get to paint! By this time, if you aren't too tired of your project, this is the most enjoyable time in the whole sequence. The paint flows on and its beauty covers the old and makes your home beautiful again. Finally, you can see the results of your work and efforts.

Now what does this have to do with *Advent*? Well, I think it is probably obvious: the preparation is *Advent* – the painting is the celebration of *Christmass*. Preparing to meet Jesus both in the Birth Event of Bethlehem and in the Final Coming involves a good bit of scraping and sanding, only we're not the painter; we're the house! The idea is — that Jesus *at his coming may find* in us *a mansion prepared for himself* – to borrow a phrase from next Sunday's *Collect*. In order for this to happen effectively, we have to lay aside our personal desires and preferences. And we must remember that keeping a mindful and watchful *Advent*, in the middle of our non-stop partying culture during December is only one way of engaging the important spiritual work of preparation. (Paraphrase of Bishop Martins' comments.)

How do our lessons for today, speak to this? First, we might look at the *Collect* for today: *The Third Sunday of Advent*:

> *Stir up your power, O Lord, and with great might come among us; and, because we are sorely hindered by our sins, let your bountiful grace and mercy speedily help and deliver us; through Jesus Christ, Our Lord, to whom, with you and the Holy Spirit, be honor and glory, now and forever. Amen.*

I mentioned last week that this *Third Sunday in Advent* is probably the forerunner of the first Mothers' Day – in England, during the Victorian era, this Sunday was called "Mothering Sunday." It was on this day, that servants were allowed to return home, often with gifts to spend some time with their families, before they returned to their employers to prepare for their sometimes very extravagant Christmass celebrations. It was also on this Sunday that in many of the more well to do families, that the father or the head of the family would formally and ceremoniously "stir up" the traditional Christmass pudding, which is actually more a cake and is probably the forerunner of today's infamous Fruit Cake. He just might add more rum or brandy – after all it might be needed to preserve the pudding to make sure it didn't spoil before Christmass!

But for us today, it is time for us to "stir up" our resolve to truly prepare ourselves during this *Advent Season*.

In our *Old Testament Lesson* from the Prophet Isaiah, we have one of the many and perhaps the most popular prophecies of the coming of the Messiah. When these events happen: the eyes of the blind are opened; the ears of the deaf unstopped; the lame leap like a deer; the tongue of the speechless sing for joy, then the Messiah has come. The Israelites knew that they had to prepare for this occurrence – they had to be ready. Then, the *Psalm* echoes the same in verse 7: *The Lord sets the prisoners free; the Lord opens the eyes of the blind; the Lord lifts up those who are bowed down.* (Psalm 146:7)

Then in our *Epistle Lesson* from the *Letter of St. James*, there is a good lesson for last Sunday's theme of *Waiting*. We are to wait, we are to be patient until the coming of the Lord.

Finally, our Gospel Lesson takes us back to John the Baptizer, who is obviously an important *Advent* character. John, now in prison, sends his disciples to Jesus to ask him if he is indeed the Messiah. Jesus tells the disciples to return to John and to tell him what they have heard and seen – the very signs of the Coming of the Messiah which we heard in our *First Lesson*. But then Jesus goes on and talks about John – John the Preparer, if you will: *See, I am sending my messenger ahead of you, who will prepare your way before you.* [Matthew 11:10]

Again, and again, we find this theme of preparation. The lives and ministries of Jesus and John were very different but there is a common theme in both their messages– the theme of repentance. Central to both is the word used both by Jesus and John – the word "repent". But the difference of John's message is the difference between the demands of a *religion of law* and the invitation to a *relationship of love*. Yet repentance properly understood is a passport to both Law and Love. Jesus set the word "repent" in the fuller context of his message of love. He didn't stop with "repent" but he went on: Believe and trust in the Gospel, the Good News of Jesus Christ; the Word Made Flesh who fulfills the Law: Jesus, who is the Way, the Truth, and the Life and who takes us all the way from Law to Love.

This is a message that we often forget and it sometimes takes a battering ram like John the Baptizer to remind us, to give us the wakeup call of *Advent*.

I would like to end this morning with the last paragraph of today's meditation from *Forward Day by Day* (Sunday,

December 15, 2013). I am continually amazed at how the right thing shows up at the right time in these meditations. I quote:

> As we prepare our hearts and our homes to celebrate Christ's birth, we have some work to do. It's not all sitting around and expecting something to happen. In our noisy culture, it means making silence. It means prayer time. Our Lord's Nativity will be celebrated in just ten days, but we have much preparation to do! Patience comes, but not without some effort. In the kingdom of God, there's not much sitting around.

There it is again: *Preparation.*

Amen

The Lectionary Page: A Liturgical Calendar for Upcoming Weeks
[www.lectionarypage.net]

- *Isaiah 35:1-10*
- *James 5:7-10*
- *Matthew 11:2-11*
- *Psalm 146:4-9*
- *or Canticle 15 [or Canticle 3*

References

Meditation for Sunday, December 15, 2013 (2013). Forward Day by Day. Cincinnati, Ohio: Forward Movement. Used by permission.

Martins, Daniel (2013). Letter from the Chair of the Board of Trustees in the *Advent Issue of the Missioner (Vol 30:2). Nashotah, Wisconsin: Nashotah House.*

Chapter Twelve
Hoping
Advent 4 [A]

In the Name of the Father, and the Son, and the Holy Spirit. Amen

When I announced this year's themes for the Candles of our *Advent Wreath*: *Anticipation, Waiting, Preparing, and Hoping*. I mentioned that the inspiration for these themes came from The Right Rev'd Daniel Martins, Bishop of Springfield, IL. He suggested these themes in in his *Letter* in the *Advent Issue of the Missioner (2013)*, a publication of Nashotah House of which Bishop Martins is the Chairman of the Board of Trustees. While I have quoted him in a few sentences and I certainly did paraphrase quite a few of his thoughts, I have not extensively quoted from his letter until today. His words on *Hope*, our *Advent Candle* theme for this *Fourth Sunday of Advent* just seemed so beautiful and appropriate, I decided to quote most of his last section. I don't think that we could possibly improve upon his words. Here it is:

> *Hoping is the jewel in the crown of the themes of our Advent vocation. Hope along with patience is one of the classic Christian moral virtues. Hope causes us to strain forward toward that which is not yet realized – we don't have it yet – but which is nonetheless grounded in reality, not something imaginary or ephemeral.* [Let me repeat that last phrase:] *Hope… we don't have it yet – but which is nonetheless grounded in reality, not something imaginary or ephemeral.* [I continue:] *The ultimate basis of our hope as Christians, of course, is the Resurrection of Christ from the dead. But there are multiple iterations of resurrection hope that virtually explode in front of us every day. Every time*

> we "keep on keeping on" when the temptation to despair seems irresistible, we are practicing the virtue of hope. As St. Paul reminds us in his letter to the Romans "For whatever was written in former days was written for our instruction, so that by steadfastness and by the encouragement of the scriptures we might have hope."

[Romans 15:4]

Bishop Martins closes his letter with this comment:

> *In the end, of all the seasons of the year, Advent is the most like real life. In our real lives, outside of liturgical time, it's always Advent. We are always waiting for a clearer revelation of God's plan and purpose. We are always preparing to put ourselves at God's disposal as heralds of his Kingdom and instruments of his peace. We are always hoping for the completion and realization of God's victory over the spiritual forces of wickedness that rebel against Him; the evil powers of this world, which corrupt and destroy the creatures of God; and the sinful desires that draw us from the love of God. In our very waiting, preparing, and hoping, we renounce them, confident that when the Son of God appears, we will "without shame or fear rejoice to behold his appearing" (Proper Prefacer of Advent) Come, Lord Jesus.*

So today, for all practical purposes, we end *Advent*; we end our anticipating, our preparing, our waiting, and our hoping. And I think there is no better way, person, or model for us to end our *Advent* than to consider the young girl of Nazareth, who with Joseph, are the subjects of today's Gospel Lesson: Mary - Mary the Virgin; Mary the Mother of our Lord and Savior Jesus Christ; Mary the God Bearer, Theotokos!

In a very real way, Mary's complete submission to God is the perfect model of hope. Let me repeat again what we said about hope a bit earlier: hope… *we don't have it yet – but which is nonetheless grounded in reality, not something imaginary or ephemeral.*

In addition, the obedience of Joseph, the patron saint of fathers as well as carpenters by the way, marks his acceptance of that hope. We must remember that both Mary and Joseph were very much aware of the "hope of the coming Messiah." This is part of the hope of their people and their faith. They did not fully know the roles that they would play or even understand them but they were willing to accept the messages of the Angels as messages from God and they accepted that reality – which was not something imaginary or ephemeral.

After the visit of the Angel in his dream: *When Joseph awoke from sleep, he did as the angel of the Lord commanded him* [Matthew 1:24] – certainly in my mind this is an action of hope and certainly it is an act of trust.

I found today's meditation in *Forward Day by Day* [Sunday, December 22, 2013. Used with Permission] a little amusing but it does offer something of importance. Let me share it with you:

A few years ago, a friend of mine was teaching an introductory class in his Episcopal congregation. The question came up, "What makes us different from Roman Catholics?" Someone piped up "We don't like Mary!" Sadly, this was not a joke.

Many Episcopalians do not give Mary much devotional attention, perhaps in reaction to other traditions where her place is quite elevated. Of course, all Christians can appreciate different facets of the same story of Christ's Incarnation, Ministry, Death, and Resurrection. That's part of the wonder and delight of the universal church.

However, I hope we can make some room for Mary, the God-bearer, in our devotional life. She literally brought God-with-us into the world, and her "yes" ranks among the most courageous acts of human history. Her faith amidst later sorrow is an inspiration for us all, knowing that God will dwell with us always. End of quote.

I will be honest, I have a special affinity for Our Lady. I do think she stands above the rest of the saints for she is the God-Bearer. I think there is something in the mysterious events surrounding the appearances of our Lady throughout history in various places and the subsequent healings connected to those appearances, many of which have been documented by physicians. As a result of these miracles and appearances, Mary has been called Our Lady of Lourdes, Our Lady of Prague, and Our Lady of Guadalupe, to mention only three occurrences. Are you also aware of our English, our Anglican Lady – Our Lady of Walsingham? The waters from the spring and well at Walsingham, England also have documented healings. Walsingham is in Norfolk County north of London. The shrine at Walsingham has long been a place of pilgrimage basically from the 11th Century. Our Lady of Walsingham is always shown seated on a throne holding a lily in her hand with the child Jesus in her lap. Right outside the entrance to the Chapel of St. Mary at Nashotah House set into the wall is a stone depiction of Our Lady of Walsingham. Perhaps this is one of the reasons for my devotion, for the House played an important and enormous role in who I am today.

But at any rate, here is a reminder: as we have said before in our discussion of the Saints, we do not pray to the Saints, we ask for their intercession in their prayers in the Community of Saints in the presence of God.

So why did I add this little excerpt about Mary into our sermon today? It is because Our Lady, Mary, along with Saint Joseph, who I think doesn't always get his due attention, are important *Advent* characters, models, and symbols. As we think back on our *Advent* themes of *Anticipation, Waiting, Preparing, and Hoping*, it is not difficult to see how both of these saints modeled in their lives the very *Advent* attributes which we have sought to find and know in our lives – not only in the anticipation of the Birth Event of Bethlehem but also in preparation for the Second Coming of Our Lord.

As I said at the beginning of this sermon, today for all practical purposes ends our *Advent* preparations, we now look forward with great eagerness and joy to *Christmass Eve* and the celebration of Our Lord's birth.

I pray that this *Advent* has not only prepared us for *Christmass* but for a greater expression of our faith; and to aid us in living a fuller Christian life.

Let us pray:

O Father, as we come to the end of this Advent Season, we pray that our Advent vocation of Anticipation, Preparation, Waiting, and Hoping has prepared us to truly meet, know, and relive the Coming of Our Lord as the Babe of Bethlehem and at the end of times as the King of All Creation. We pray that our hearts and lives have been changed so that we may live a life of service to you and to your people. Hear us, O Lord, as we pray in the name of our Lord and Savior, Jesus Christ.

Amen

The Lectionary Page: A Liturgical Calendar for Upcoming Weeks
[www.lectionarypage.net]

- *Isaiah 7:10-16*
- *Romans 1:1-7*
- *Matthew 1:18-25*
- *Psalm 80:1-7, 16-18*

References

Martins, Daniel (2013). Letter from the Chair of the Board of Trustees in the *Advent Issue of the Missioner (Vol 30:2)*. Nashotah, Wisconsin: Nashotah House.

Meditation for Sunday, December 22, 2013 (2013). *Forward Day by Day*. Cincinnati, Ohio: Forward Movement.

Addendum
Advent Customs and Traditions

This is by no means an exhaustive list of Advent Customs and Traditions but rather it is intended to be a starting place for you as you seek to enrich your Advent Preparations and Celebrations. With our modern technology, you can easily find many more practices and variations of these practices.

The Advent Wreath

Perhaps the most well know Advent Tradition is the Advent Wreath. The history is uncertain but what does exist is interesting and there is indication that the Advent Wreath has been used since Medieval Times. The circular wreath reminds us that God has no beginning and no end: Alpha and Omega. The greenery reminds us of God's everlasting love, the promise of eternal life, and our ever-growing faith. The four candles, one for each of the *Sundays of Advent*, reminds us that we are watching and preparing for our King. They also represent Jesus' overcoming the darkness of hatred and evil with the light of joy and love. On the *Fourth Sunday of Advent*, when all four candles are burning brightly, we are reminded that Jesus changed darkness into the light of joy and love. The ever-increasing light of the Advent Wreath – candles growing steadily shorter, light growing steadily brighter mirrors our growing anticipation and heralds the ever, nearer presence of Christ, our light and our salvation. On *Christmass Eve*, we light the *Christ Candle*, representing his Presence in the world.

Over the years, additional meanings have been added to the Advent Wreath and traditionally, we have given names to the candles. A common tradition is to name the candles in this way: The *First Week of Advent*: The Prophecy Candle; *The Second Week of Advent*: The Bethlehem Candle; *The Third Week of Advent*: The Shepherds' Candle; and *The Fourth Week of Advent*: The Angels' Candle. For the most part, but not always, the naming of these candles parallels the appointed Scripture lessons for each Sunday in *Advent*.

Other traditions have named the candles in this way: *The First Candle*: The Promise of the Second Coming; *The Second Candle*: The Candle of the Prophecy concerning John the Baptizer; *The Third Candle*: The Candle of John as Messenger; and *the Fourth Candle*: The Birth or Bethlehem Candle. Other naming traditions exist as well and some are mentioned above in this collection of sermons.

The color of the candles also represents different traditions. Perhaps the most common is the Latin Rite: three purple candles and one rose or pink candle (for the Third Sunday in Advent). Two English customs are to use all purple or all white. In some places, during the Twelve Days of Christmas, all of the candles are replaced with white candles. Becoming more popular today is the use of blue candles, which reflects the Sarum Rite from the Cathedral of York in England. All red candles are a Bavarian tradition. I like to change the color of candles from year to year.

There are also various prayers that are used with the Advent Wreath both in church and at home. Some are more elaborate, some more simple. One set of prayers that I like can be found on The Episcopal Church Foundation web site, which also has links to various other Advent customs. http://www.ecfvp.org/tools/advent-resources/

You can find an interesting history of the Advent Wreath at:

http://www.catholiceducation.org/en/culture/catholic-contributions/the-history-of-the-advent-wreath.html

The Chrismons Tree

A popular and growing practice is the Chrismons Tree, which was started by Lutherans, for which we are grateful.

What are Chrismons?

These are ornaments made from Christian symbols (or Chrismons, a contraction for Christ monograms) were first developed by Frances Spencer and the women of the Ascension Lutheran Church in Danville, Virginia. Many churches display a Chrismons tree during the Advent and Christmas season decorated with handmade ornaments. In my practice, we have encouraged families to make the Chrismons either in the parish hall or at home and we add one or two each Sunday to the tree, which is placed in the Sanctuary. Patterns are provided. The Chrismons are usually all in white, gold, and silver. This makes a beautiful tree and color can be added on *Christmass Eve*.

For more information visit:
https://www.whychristmas.com/customs/chrismons.shtml

There are several books available on Chrismons. Here are some books that I can recommend:

Spencer, Frances Kipps (1965) *CHRISMONS, Three Volumes (Basic Series, Advanced Series, and Christian Year Series).* Danville, VA: The Lutheran Church of Ascension.

Huwiler, Beth; Ellen Hohenfeldt; and Diane Weaver. (1977) Chrismons *for Your Tree: Christian Ornaments for Home and Church.* Colorado Springs CO: Ideals Children's Books.

Advent Calendars

Advent Calendars are especially popular with younger children. There are many commercial examples available. Basically, they are usually standing pictures on which there are twenty-four doors. On each day of *Advent*, one of the doors is opened. There are two types: one when the door is opened will have a Scripture verse that over *Advent* these verses tell the Christmass Story. The other shows a picture or symbol about which the child may make up a story. This is great for participation and encouraging creativity. Placing a candle behind the Calendar will show through the doors and further illuminate the pictures or Scripture verses.

The Procession of the Nativity Set

This custom may not be so widely known, but it was a favorite of my son when he was young. On the *First Sunday of Advent*, the crèche is put in its place, where it will remain during the *Christmass Season.* The rest of the figures are placed on a table near the front door. Then on each *Sunday of Advent*, the figures are moved closer to the crèche. Depending upon the figures in your Nativity Set and the number of figures, this usually requires at least two or three stations. The idea is that the figures are slowly moving to the crèche and on the *Fourth Sunday of Advent* they are all in place at the crèche. For example, on the *Second Sunday of*

Advent, the animals are moved to Station Two. On the *Third Sunday of Advent*, they are moved to Station Three and the shepherds are moved to Station Two. The figures progress until on *Christmass Eve*, the Christ Child is placed in the crèche and a Christ Candle is lit. We always did this on Sunday nights right before we lit our Advent Candle at our evening meal.

The intention of these customs, practices, and traditions are to involve are minds and thoughts, and even our bodies, in our *Advent Preparations*. They should be done in such a way that the impact of a commercial *Christmass* is reduced. I encourage you to work with your own families and create your own *Advent Customs*. I promise you, your preparations for the Celebration of Our Lord's Birth on *Christmass Day* will be enriched.

God bless you and have a Holy Advent.

www.ingramcontent.com/pod-product-compliance
Lightning Source LLC
Chambersburg PA
CBHW052116110526
44592CB00013B/1627